INDIVIDUALIZED SPELLING

Spelling Activities for a Balanced Reading Program

By
Jillayne Prince Wallaker

Inside Illustrations by
Barb Lorseyedi

Cover Illustration by
Vickie Lane

Publishers
Instructional Fair • TS Denison
Grand Rapids, Michigan 49544

Permission to Reproduce

Instructional Fair • TS Denison grants the right to the individual purchaser to reproduce patterns and student activity materials in this book for noncommercial individual or classroom use only. Reproduction for an entire school or school system is strictly prohibited. No other part of this publication may be reproduced in whole or in part. No part of this publication may be reproduced for storage in a retrieval system, or transmitted in any form or by any means, electronic, mechanical, recording, or otherwise, without the prior written permission of the publisher. For information regarding permission write to: Instructional Fair • TS Denison, P.O. Box 1650, Grand Rapids, MI 49501.

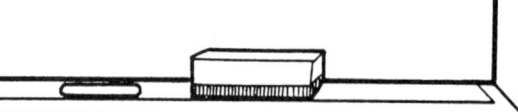

Dedication
With love to Maegen Mikaela

Credits
Author: Jillayne Prince Wallaker
Inside Illustrations: Barb Lorseyedi
Project Director/Editor: Elizabeth Flikkema
Editors: Alyson Kieda, Rhonda DeWaard
Cover Artist: Vickie Lane
Production: Pat Geasler

About the Author
Jillayne Prince Wallaker has been teaching in grades one through three for over 12 years in Michigan. Mrs. Wallaker earned her bachelor of science degree and a master's degree from Grand Valley State University where she also taught a graduate level elementary mathematics course. Jillayne enjoys writing curriculum and supplemental books for teachers.

Standard Book Number 1-56822-468-0
Individualized Spelling–Primary
© 1997 by Instructional Fair • TS Denison
2400 Turner NW
Grand Rapids, MI 49544

All Rights Reserved • Printed in the USA

Table of Contents

Introduction (4-5)
Individualizing Your Spelling Program (5)

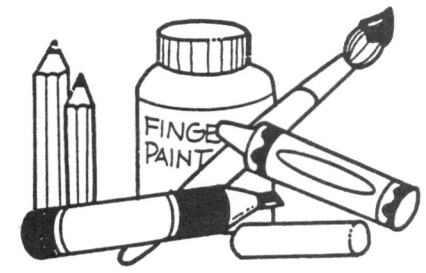

Repetition Activities
Notes to the Teacher (6-10)

Alphabet Soup	11
Bag-It	11
Beans	12
Circles	12
BINGO	13
Clap-Tap Spelling	14
Colored Specks	14
Colored Vowels	15
Cookie Cutters	15
Decorate It	16
Dice-Roll Rainbow	16
Fabric Scraps	17
Fingerpaint Words	17
Floor to Ceiling	18
Four-Column Spelling	18
Four-Minute Spelling	19
Hands On!	19
Jump Rope	20
Junk Mail Letters	20
Listening Center I	21
Listening Center II	22
Magnetic Letters	23
Musical Spelling	23
Paint with Water	24
Paper Punch	24
Race to Draw	25
Read, Write, and Spell	25
Sandpaper Spelling	26
Scrambled Words	26
Scramble, Unscramble I and II	27
Sidewalk Chalk	28
Silly Voices	28
Snakes and Worms	29
Spelling Cards	29
Spelling Stairs	30
Spiral It	30
Squirt Bottle	31
Stamp Pad Letters	31
String It Along	32
Texture Writing	32
Typewriter	33
Word Shapes	33
Write It on . . .	34
Write It with . . .	34
Writing on the Wall	35

Context-Based Activities
Notes to the Teacher (36)

ABC	37
Dictionary Cards and Sentences	37
Flip-Check	38
Flip Up, Fill in the Blank	38
Photo Captions	39
Relationships	39
Teach a Word	40

Management

Pretest	41
I Know These Words	42
Daily Recording Chart	43
Spelling Words to Practice	43
Weekly Recording Chart	44
Spelling Test	45
My Spelling List	46
BINGO	47
Grid Paper	48

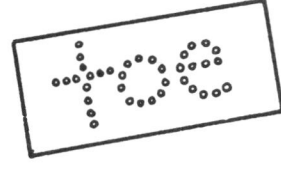

Introduction

Individualized Spelling is designed to teach spelling in a balanced reading program. When spelling lists arise out of class work and student writing, teachers may find it difficult to design activities that the whole class can use. The activities in this book can be used with any list of spelling words. Even if teachers are using an existing spelling program, they may use *Individualized Spelling* activities as a supplement. The varied activities are student-centered and address the styles of most learners.

Learning to spell involves practice and repetition. Pages 11-35 contain over 40 interesting and fun repetition activities, utilizing many learning styles. Since it is also important for students to learn more than the words' spellings, the activities on pages 37–40 require students to use their spelling words in meaningful contexts. For an extended resource of context-based spelling activities, refer to *Individualized Spelling, Intermediate Level*, the next book in this series.

Each activity is written in an easy-to-read format that can be reproduced. The directions are simple enough for the self-directed primary reader. The activity sheets may be reproduced for homework or for the parent desiring work for a child going on an extended vacation. They are ideally suited for volunteers or cross-grade tutors to follow. Teacher information and further directions for preparation, alphabetized by activity name, precede each section of activities. Refer to these when choosing activities to present to students. You will also find reproducible test pages, blank data recording charts, and other management pages at the back of the book. Use them to tailor your own Individualized Spelling program.

Suggested Procedure

✦ Give a pretest (see p. 41) on Thursday. Students are more likely to study spelling on the weekend when they have already spent two days on a list of words and their level of concern has been raised sufficiently. The pretest tells students which words require the most practice and therefore the most repetition activities.

✦ After the pretest, students write their individual lists on p. 46 or on the Weekly Recording Chart (p. 44). The teacher then models and provides materials for up to 10 spelling activities. The majority of activities will be repetition (taken from pp. 11-35) but also include one to three context-based activities (pp. 37-40). The teacher may write the activity names on the Activity Choices section of the Weekly Recording Chart before duplicating or provide a menu from which students may choose. The menu of activities can grow over the weeks as the students become familiar with them. Write your own routines among the activity choices, such as copying the list for homework. Each activity is paired with a letter at the bottom of p. 44.

✦ On Thursday and Friday, students practice their spelling words using some of the repetition and context-based activities listed on the recording chart. On one of the nine spaces following the spelling word, students write the letters assigned to the activities used. Alternatively, use the Daily Recording Chart (p. 43) with a different activity each day.

◆ On Monday and Tuesday, continue to use a variety of activities, but begin to focus on the words that students most often misspell. Students may use the chart on the bottom of page 43 to keep track of the words that need extra practice.

✦ On Wednesday, if time permits, allow students to complete one repetition activity before the final test. After the test, have the students write the words they mastered in a **I Know These Words** booklet (see p. 42). The misspelled words may be listed on a page labelled, "words-to-learn." Optional: you may wish to provide students with an opportunity to practice the next list before the pretest.

Introduction

Individualizing Your Spelling Program

Give all your students the same list on the pretest day. After correcting their own tests, allow students to replace already mastered words with words from their personal writing, their "words-to-learn" list, or the current unit of study. Students should write their individualized list twice—one list for themselves and another for the teacher. The teacher then keeps a running list of the students' individual words. After students have mastered words, the teacher holds students accountable for those words in their writing and daily work.

Have students maintain a "words-to-learn" list. They can add words to this list from their daily writing, missed words on spelling tests, or the current topic of study. Cross any words mastered off the "words to learn" list and add them to a dictionary (see **I Know These Words** p. 42).

Give students with less ability a partial list by asking that they write every other word on the test. This allows them to take the test along with the other students without feeling left out. They also have more time for each word without holding up the rest of the class. Alternatively, give these students a separate list such as basic sight words. Test them while the other students are doing repetition activities.

High-ability students who pass the pretest may use an alternative list. Since they have passed your curriculum list, highlight the appropriate box in the teacher's record book with a green marker (green for go on to another list). The score of the bonus list can be recorded over the green marker. Allow these students to choose 10 to 16 words from their writing or the current unit of study. This group does all the same class activities, but with their own list. On test day, allow them to give each other the test while you give the group test. In this case, the teacher corrects their tests. Any words not mastered go onto the next alternate spelling list. Students can record these on a "words-to-learn" list.

If you would like individual lists for every student, try this management alternative. Provide one yearly spelling list that all students work their way through. Give five individual spelling tests each day while the other students are working on spelling activities with their own lists. Students progress at their own pace and add words from their writing throughout the year or when they finish the provided list.

Enjoy exploring spelling as you use the activities in this book, along with your own individualized ideas.

🍎 Materials

Many of the activities in this book call for materials. Write a note to parents requesting some of the following items: empty boxes (cereal, etc.), junk mail and envelopes, macaroni, string, yarn, empty bottles (dishwashing liquid, contact solution, etc.), play dough, letter-shaped cookie cutters, wallpaper, gift wrap, items with interesting textures, resealable bags, dried beans, dice, sidewalk chalk, fabric, magazines, magnetic letters, sandpaper, trays, old cake pans, musical instruments (percussion), and an old typewriter.

© Instructional Fair • TS Denison — IF5091 Individualized Spelling–Primary

Notes to the Teacher

Repetition Activities

Students need to use repetition activities in order to master spelling words. Since there are many activities to choose from, select a limited number of these activities, gather the materials and model the procedures, and then let students choose from those options. Each week make sure that students have access to activities that stimulate their different intelligences such as verbal, visual, musical, and kinesthetic. The information below will help you choose and prepare for the best activities for your students and will refer you to the corresponding sheet of student directions. For each activity, every student will need a copy of his/her spelling list or one of the recording charts (p. 43 or 44).

🍎 **Alphabet Soup** (p. 11) Students have fun manipulating this unlikely medium. This activity also develops fine motor skills. The words will show up dramatically if students arrange the white pasta letters on a dark background. If students cannot find a needed letter, allow them to write it on a small scrap of paper. The idea is not to spend hours on this activity, but to learn the spelling words. If you would like students to glue the pasta letters down after they have formed the word, provide them with thick paper and glue.

As an alternative, color the pasta ahead of time using the following recipe. Pour the box of uncooked macaroni into a gallon-sized resealable bag, add 5 to 10 drops of food coloring and 3 tbsp. rubbing alcohol. Seal the bag and shake until all the pieces are coated. Open and pour the pasta onto several layers of newspaper to dry. Store in resealable containers or a plastic bag. As an option, students may use one color for vowels and another for the consonants. Or, they may use different colors for combinations you are working on such as digraphs, blends, or suffixes.

Another option is to use alphabet cereal instead of the pasta. It is more expensive but the letters are larger and a little easier to manipulate.

🍎 **Bag-It** (p. 11) provides tactile learners with a squishy but clean way to practice their spelling words. Prepare the bags by filling quart-sized resealable bags with anything squishy: pudding, thick tempera paint, shampoo, liquid dish soap, and so on. Place 1/2 cup of goo in one bag. Squeeze out any extra air and seal. Place the first bag into a second bag, the same size or larger. Seal the second bag. For extra security, seal the outside bag with heavy duty tape.

🍎 **Beans** (p. 12) is a good activity to use with a list containing words with similar letter patterns. When students find a repeated sequence of letters, they can use the same bean configuration for more than one word, thus saving time. It does not take students long to figure this strategy out! Any type of dried bean can be used. However, on a light-colored desk, dark-brown lima beans work best. On a dark surface, white beans work best. Alternatives to beans include small objects such as buttons, cereal, colored rice, macaroni shapes, or holiday candy (an educational option for your class party).

🍎 **BINGO** (p. 13) is a game that can be played by students with the same spelling list or during review weeks. Make the cards from any type of paper. Cut the paper into same-sized pieces, just large enough to hold a handwritten spelling word. (One option is to cut 3" x 5" cards into fourths.) The game can be played by the whole class, in small groups, or with partners. Use dyed pasta, small blocks, or beans in place of BINGO chips.

If a single list is used, write some words in more than one box. Since the word will be on the BINGO worksheet more than once, teachers must emphasize the rule that once a box is covered, it cannot be traded for a different box with the same word. Also, for each word drawn, only one box on the worksheet may be covered.

Students with individualized lists can play this game by writing their extra words on cards and adding their words to those already in the bag.

Extension: Once a word is drawn, students give a definition, riddle, or other clue rather than simply spelling the word.

🍎 **Circles** (p. 12) is a fun activity that gives students tactile practice going over the shapes of the letters that make up each spelling word. Several students may share a stamp pad.

Notes to the Teacher

- **Clap-Tap Spelling** (p. 14) provides auditory and kinesthetic learners with sound and touch cues for each letter in the word. Use this activity with the whole group, a small group, or individual students. Use the paper from **Colored Vowels** (p. 15) as a guide for students or write the words on the recording chart, marking the vowels with a separate color.

- **Colored Specks** (p. 14) is an activity for tactile and visual learners. Provide containers of at least two different colors of sand, smashed macaroni, crushed cereal, glitter, or other small items. (Color sand by adding chalk or tempera paint powder.) Have students work over newspaper or a lipped tray or box. Show students ahead of time how to glue, sprinkle, and save sand to promote neatness and conserve materials. As an alternative, work outside and use two colors of glue. Sprinkle with sand.

- **Colored Vowels** (p. 15) highlights the vowels or vowel combinations present in spelling words. Use this activity to reinforce decoding skills used in reading and writing. Be sure to inform students when special vowel combinations are present. Tactile learners can lightly rub a finger over the word to feel the vowels.

- **Cookie Cutters** (p. 15) provides students with the opportunity to handle play dough while they learn their spelling words. If you do not have access to alphabet cookie cutters, have students lay tagboard letter cutouts on the play dough and cut around them with a plastic knife. Commercial or homemade play dough work equally well. Use an old rolling pin or an unbreakable cylinder to roll out the dough.

- **Decorate It** (p. 16) appeals to artistic students. It gives them the opportunity to decorate the letters by doodling or to make a picture representing the word. This activity also has the visual learner studying the shape of the letters and word repeatedly.

- **Dice-Roll Rainbow** (p. 16) requires the student to write each word several times. Rolling the die to determine the number of times the word is traced gives the activity a game-like character. Insist that the students trace the entire word with one color before starting with the next color. This allows them to learn the configuration of the whole word.

- **Fabric Scraps** (p. 17) provides a variety of textures for tactile learners to trace on, and it is a handy way to use extra fabric or old clothing. Precut fabric into pieces large enough to hold a single spelling word or a full list. The scrap cardboard under the fabric keeps markers from bleeding through to the desk or table top.

- **Fingerpaint Words** (p. 17) is great for tactile learners. You can use tempera paint or a stamp pad, but watercolor paint cleans up the easiest.

- **Floor to Ceiling** (p. 18) appeals to the visual learner by helping the student to picture the word in his/her head. It also allows the student to practice words without using a writing utensil. Use 3" x 5" index or similar cards to write the spelling words on.

- **Four-Column Spelling** (p.18) is great for the intrapersonal learner, allowing students to practice independently and to self-correct. Show the students how to fold the paper so that there are four columns. For an extension, have students leave a space between words and write a sentence below each of the spelling words.

- **Four-Minute Spelling** (p. 19) can be practiced by the entire class at one time. The goal is to write the spelling words correctly as many times as possible in four minutes, repeating the list as necessary. Generate enthusiasm for working quickly and accurately by setting goals or awarding prizes. Students work in teams of two: one acts as teacher, the other writes his/her words as they are dictated. After four minutes the students switch roles. Before they begin, model and discuss how partners should play their roles—the "teacher" saying "good job" or "that's not right." Students become aware of which words they need to practice because those words slow them down.

Notes to the Teacher

Have students record their **Four-Minute Spelling** score on their recording chart. Each day they should look for an increase in their score. Give a star or sticker each day the score improves. Use the four-minute concept to help students memorize math facts as well!

- **Hands On!** (p. 19) Start with a 9" x 13" pan, a lunch tray, or other rectangular container with sides. Fill the pan with flour, pudding, shaving cream, shampoo, a thick liquid, a powder, or another substance that will retain an impression. Do not use scented or powdery items if you have any students with asthma or allergies. You might use a pan of snow in the winter or a tray of sand in the fall or spring for this tactile experience.

- **Jump Rope** (p. 20) is a kinesthetic, large-motor activity. This activity is appealing to the child who does not like to use writing utensils. Use a long rope with two students twirling so the jumper can hold a spelling list. To easily identify the vowels, trace them with a crayon. Students jumping alone can write the words on a chalkboard or paper large enough to see while jumping.

Students who cannot jump rope and participate in a spelling activity at the same time can jump in place. For your very coordinated students, combine this activity with **Clap-Tap Spelling** (p. 14).

- **Junk Mail Letters** (p. 20) demonstrates that spelling is a real-life activity. It also creates an awareness of ways to reuse paper before recycling. You will have no problems finding parents to provide the materials for this activity. Students may place a check over each letter in the spelling word they have located in order to keep track of the letters that still need to be found. When students complete their lists, place a sticker over the stamp on the front. Or provide stickers, stamps, or rubber stamps so that students can stamp each others' work.

- **Listening Center I and II** (pp. 21-22) is a great activity for students who love to talk or act. This activity also allows students to use and develop listening skills. You may assign one or two students to do the taping for students who are unable to create their own tape. Teach students how to use the tape recorder before you assign this activity. **Listening Center I** creates a tape that students can use for independent practice. **Listening Center II** is ideal for auditory learners and teaches the spelling words through repetition as students follow along.

- **Magnetic Letters** (p. 23) Provide students with an appropriate surface such as a cookie sheet, the side of their desk, a filing cabinet, or a chalkboard. If you do not have magnetic letters, use any premade alphabet letters for this activity.

- **Musical Spelling** (p. 23) is a wonderful activity for the musical/rhythmic student who remembers things set to music. If the two musical notes have a wide range, the sounds, along with the vowel and consonant placement, may be recalled at test time. "Music makers" could include a piano, keyboard, xylophone, a toy that makes more than one noise, or another musical instrument that is played with the hands. Homemade rubber band boxes can also be used if the tension on the two bands allows students to play two very different notes. Percussion instruments such as drums, tambourines, cymbals, maracas, castanets, and rattles also work well.

- **Paint with Water** (p. 24), a kinesthetic activity, requires very few materials and students love it. Before you begin, make sure that water will not damage your chalkboard. If a chalkboard is not available, use a door, wall, or sidewalk that is water-safe for this activity. **Hint:** For water marks that linger, erase with a chalkboard eraser.

- **Paper Punch** (p. 24) is a visual and kinesthetic activity. Experiment with the given paper size and cut the paper to fit the needs of your students. Model this activity for students before you assign it as independent work. Make sure students write the individual letters large enough to punch over. You might glue the completed word onto a contrasting color of paper and display the finished product on a bulletin board.

Notes to the Teacher

- **Race to Draw** (p. 25) is a more positive version of the game of "Hangman" in which partners race to be the first to complete a drawing. Rather than work with one word and fill in letters, this game calls for the entire word to be spelled correctly. This can be played with partners or in teams.

  Before the game begins, students must agree on the object to be drawn and an exact number of steps required to complete the drawing.

- **Read, Write, and Spell** (p. 25) is very useful for learners of all styles. Auditory learners hear the words as they are spelled and traced three times each. Visual learners see the words as they are written and erased. Tactile learners feel each word as it is first spelled with chalk and then traced with the pointer finger. **Read, Write, and Spell** is effective as a whole-class, teacher-directed activity or can be used with small groups or student partners.

- **Sandpaper Spelling** (p. 26) is a wonderful activity for tactile learners. An adult should write the spelling words on the sandpaper with a permanent marker ahead of time. For students with poor vision, use a crayon instead of marker. The student may follow the crayon on his/her own, or have another student lead his/her index finger while the two students say each letter.

- **Scrambled Words** (p. 26) is a student-made, self-checking center activity. This activity calls students' attention to individual letters in the spelling words as they make their own scrambled word cards. Use 3" x 5" index cards for this activity.

- **Scramble, Unscramble** (p. 27) provides students with the opportunity to analyze each word. This two-part activity appeals to verbal/linguistic and logical/mathematical learners. For a simpler activity have the students place only one scrambled word in an envelope. If you have a student who is an especially neat writer, you can laminate his/her grid paper before cutting to provide a permanent class game. Another option is to have the students glue the letters down after they have been unscrambled. Junk mail envelopes are perfect for holding the scrambled letters in this activity.

- **Sidewalk Chalk** (p. 28) is both a new and fun way for students to write their lists and an academic excuse to use the wonderful outside classroom. Take the whole class outside or ask a volunteer to take a small group of students. If you have colored chalk, you might combine this activity with **Dice-Roll Rainbow** (p, 16). Roll the dice to find out with how many colors each word must be traced. Or, use two colors of chalk and follow the directions for **Colored Vowels** (p. 19).

- **Silly Voices** (p. 28) allows students to have fun with their voices and it exercises their verbal and musical intelligences. **Silly voices** works well for teams of two students. It is an activity best done when the teacher's tolerance for noise is high. Go outside to do this activity on a sunny day. Try it as a group activity when all are using the same list of words and the same voices. Add as many types of voices as you can dream up.

- **Snakes and Worms** (p. 29) uses play dough worms or snakes to form spelling words. This is an ideal activity for tactile learners or students who have an aversion to paper and pencil work. Purchase Play-Doh or use the following recipe to make your own play dough: 1 cup salt, 2 cups sifted flour, 6 teaspoons alum (found in spice aisle), 2 tablespoons salad oil, and 1 cup water. Mix together until smooth. Coloring may be added to the water before mixing. The play dough will stay soft for weeks if kept in a sealed plastic bag (longer in the refrigerator).

  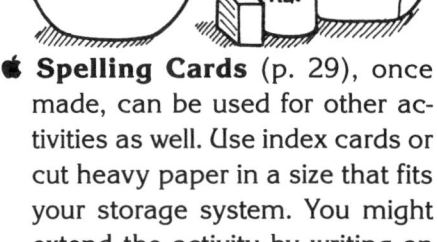

- **Spelling Cards** (p. 29), once made, can be used for other activities as well. Use index cards or cut heavy paper in a size that fits your storage system. You might extend the activity by writing an example sentence or a definition on the back of the card and filing the cards in alphabetical order.

- **Spelling Stairs** (p. 30) helps students see the word in a part-to-whole relationship. Visual learners are provided with a shape and size. Allow tactile learners to cut out the staircase. To create the staircase, first letters must be written in the same vertical column, adding one letter each time.

  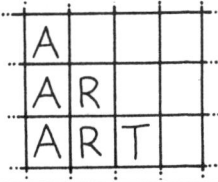

Notes to the Teacher

❦ **Spiral It** (p. 30) is an activity for the kinesthetic intelligence. Draw the letters on paper using crayons or on a chalkboard using chalk. For large motor development, students can write very large letters on the chalkboard. Students will have fun using any paper available. Teach students how to spiral a letter. Form the spiral letter in the same direction as you would for penmanship. Start at the beginning of the letter and make continuous circles (spirals) throughout the letter.

❦ **Squirt Bottle** (p. 31) can be used on a sidewalk, in dirt, or in the snow. Give careful and strict instructions about appropriate use of the water in this activity. Some bottles that work well are liquid dishwashing soap bottles, sample-size shampoo or baby oil bottles, and contact solution bottles. When working in snow, add food coloring to the water to brighten the letters. You might use this activity after **Sidewalk Chalk** (p. 28). Squirt over each chalk letter and help clean the sidewalk.

❦ **Stamp Pad Letters** (p. 31) gives students another medium with which to spell their words. To make your own alphabet stamps, purchase an inexpensive set of alphabet erasers and glue them upside down to wooden cubes or to the bottoms of pill bottles. Or, purchase craft foam, cut out letters, and glue them onto caps from milk bottles.

❦ **String It Along** (p. 32) is an activity in which students manipulate pieces of string, yarn, ribbon, or cord to form each letter. Prepare a box of string cut into 8" to 12" lengths. As an alternative, you might combine this activity with **Colored Vowels** (p. 15) by having students form consonants in one color and vowels in another color of string.

❦ **Texture Writing** (p. 32) helps learners memorize the "feel" of each word. It also creates a visual image of the words. Use lightweight paper over the textured surface. If the paper is too thick, students will not easily feel the texture below. To make homemade sandpaper, brush a heavyweight paper (tag board or a cereal box) with a thin layer of glue and sprinkle sand over it. Let it dry thoroughly. Other textured surfaces include a sidewalk, a floor mat, a spackled wall, the grate on the heat register, lunch trays, or a basket. Encourage the students to look around for more ideas!

❦ **Typewriter** (p. 33) is an activity students love. Teach students how to load the paper, use the space bar, and advance to the next line.

❦ **Word Shapes** (p. 33) provides visual learners with an exaggerated shape for each spelling word. Students compare and memorize shapes, sizes, and lengths of words. You might combine this activity with **Colored Vowels** (p. 15) or **Dice-Roll Rainbow** (p. 16) to provide reinforcement. If you have a student who cannot make the shapes, draw the outline ahead of time on the grid paper and allow the student to fill in the shapes.

❦ **Write It on . . .** (p. 34) Students love choices! For this activity, allow students to choose what they will write on. Options include lined paper, construction paper, wallpaper, newspaper, aluminum foil, gift wrap, chalkboard, and scraps of lamination film. Use an appropriate writing tool for the chosen writing surface.

❦ **Write It with . . .** (p. 34) is an activity that allows students to choose a variety of writing tools to copy their lists. Have some of these available: crayons, paintbrushes and paint, finger paint, markers, pens, colored pencils, and chalk.

❦ **Writing on the Wall** (p. 35) uses a teacher's tool—the overhead projector. Teach students how to use the overhead projector first. *Hint:* Place a transparency with writing lines under a clear transparency. This promotes neatness, and the lines stay on the projector for the next student while the first student cleans the top transparency.

teacher notes p. 6

Alphabet Soup

Materials: alphabet-shaped pasta and a pencil

Directions:

1. Choose a spelling word. Say it.
2. Sort through the pasta to find each letter needed for this word.
3. Spell the word on the table with pasta letters.
4. Find a partner and say and spell the word for that person.
5. Repeat for each spelling word.

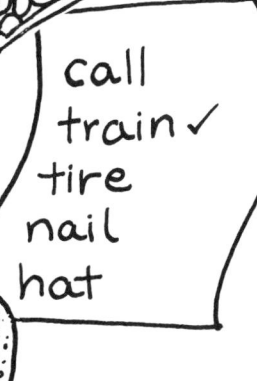

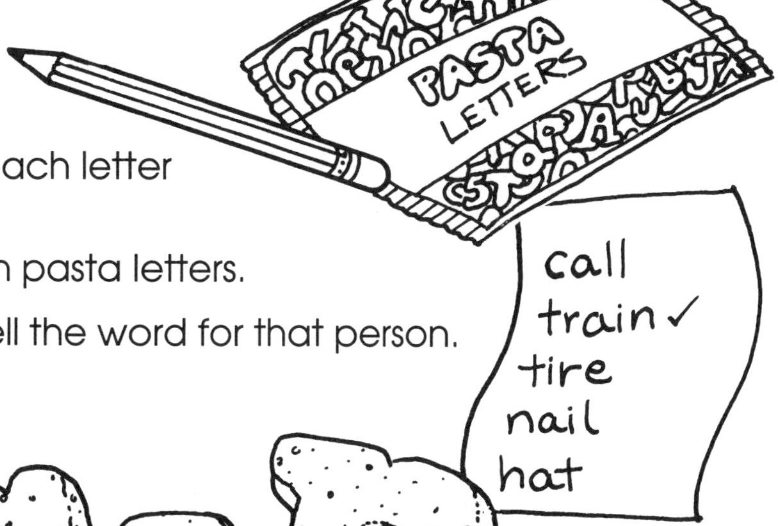
PASTA
LETTERS
call
train ✓
tire
nail
hat

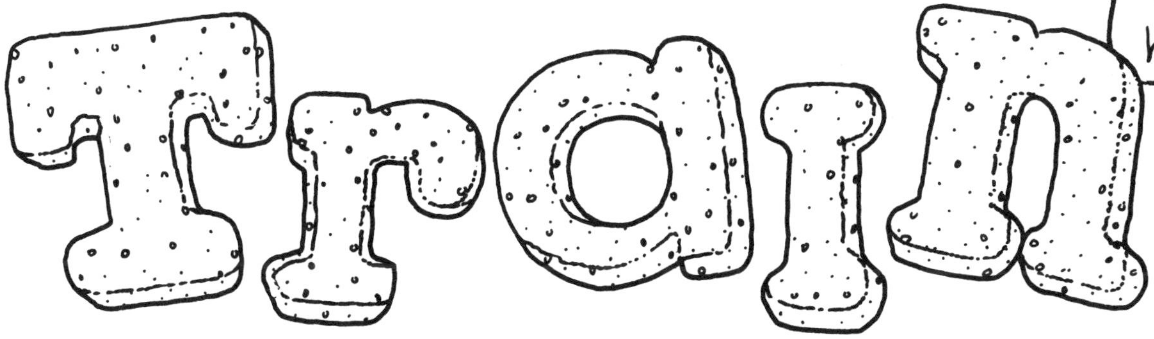
Train

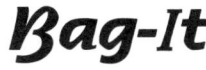

teacher notes p. 6

Bag-It

Materials: a bag of squishy stuff

Directions:

1. Work with a partner. Lay the bag on a smooth, clean surface away from any sharp objects. Do not open the bags.
2. Choose a spelling word. Say it.
3. With your finger, write the word into the goo through the bag. As you "write" each letter, say it out loud with your partner.
4. Allow your partner to have a turn, again saying the letters together.
5. Choose another word and repeat.

c

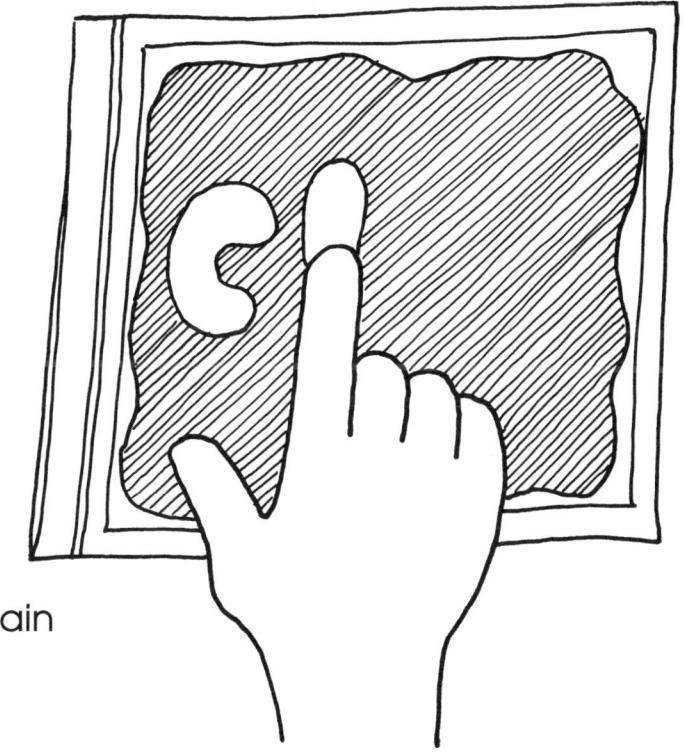

teacher notes p. 6

Beans

Materials: your spelling list and a container of dried beans

Directions:

1. Choose a spelling word. Say the word.
2. Look at the word. Place beans on the table in the shape of each letter of the word.
3. After you have spelled the word with beans, find a partner.
4. Say the word to your partner. Spell the word, pointing to the letters of the word. Then say the word again.
5. Repeat for each of your spelling words.

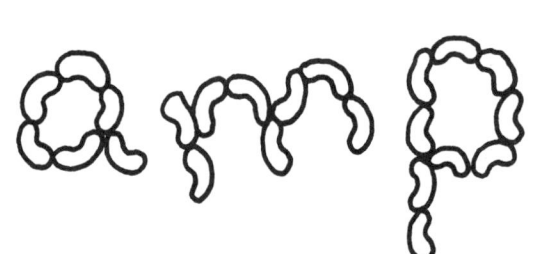

teacher notes p. 6

Circles

Materials: plain paper, a pencil with a new eraser, and a stamp pad

Directions:

1. Choose a spelling word. Say it.
2. Write the word in large letters on your paper.
3. Press your pencil eraser onto the stamp pad.
4. Trace each letter with prints made by your eraser.
5. Repeat for each spelling word.

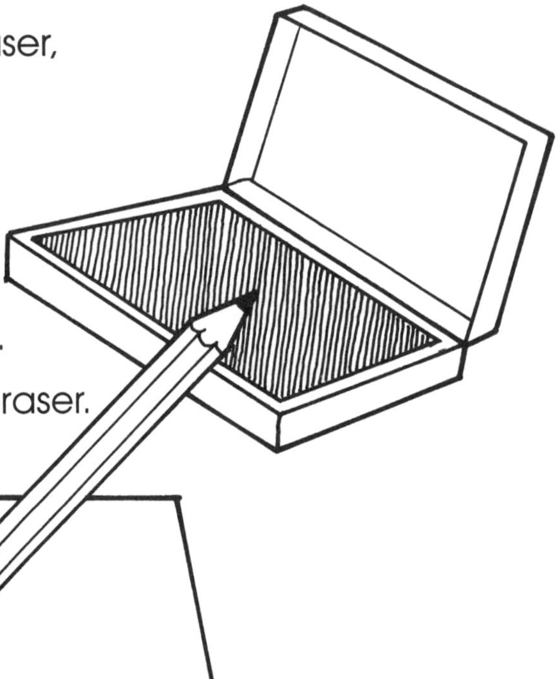

© Instructional Fair • TS Denison   12   IF5091 *Individualized Spelling–Primary*

teacher notes p. 6

BINGO

Preparing the game

Materials: the BINGO worksheet (p. 47), precut cards, a paper lunch bag, and a pencil

Directions:

1. Choose a spelling word. Say it.
2. Copy the word neatly on any line of the BINGO worksheet. Say each letter.
3. Repeat until each spelling word has been copied and the worksheet is filled. You may need to use some spelling words twice.
4. Write one spelling word on each of the precut cards. Write each word only once. Put the words in a lunch bag.

Playing the game

Materials: completed BINGO worksheets, completed spelling cards in a lunch bag, and BINGO chips

Directions:

1. The caller picks a card, looks at the word, and says the word for all to hear.
2. The other players repeat and spell the word in unison. Each player places a BINGO chip over the word once on the worksheet. **Note:** once a box is chosen, it cannot be changed during that game. Then the caller shows the card. The other players look at the card and trace the word in the air while spelling it out loud.
3. The caller returns the card to the bag.
4. Another player becomes the caller, chooses a card, and repeats steps 1–3.
5. The game continues until one person gets BINGO, which is four chips in a row—horizontally, vertically, or diagonally.

© Instructional Fair • TS Denison 13 IF5091 *Individualized Spelling–Primary*

Clap-Tap Spelling

teacher notes p. 7

Materials: your spelling list

Directions:

1. Choose a spelling word. Say the word.
2. Look at the word and decide which letters are consonants. You will clap these letters.
3. Decide which letters are vowels. You will tap these letters on your knee or on your desk.
4. Say each letter of the word as you clap the consonants and tap the vowels.
5. Say the word again.
6. Repeat three times for each word.
7. Choose another spelling word and begin again.

"and   a – n – d   and"
            tap   clap   clap

teacher notes p. 7

Colored Specks

Materials: heavy paper, glue, colored sand, and a pencil

Directions:

1. Choose a spelling word and write it in large letters on the paper.
2. Carefully trace the vowels with liquid glue.
3. Sprinkle one color of sand over the gluey vowels.
4. Follow teacher directions for saving colored specks.
5. Carefully trace the consonants with glue.
6. Sprinkle a different color of sand over the gluey consonants and save the colored specks.
8. Find a friend and say the word. Point to each letter as you spell it. Then say the word again.
9. Repeat for each of your spelling words.

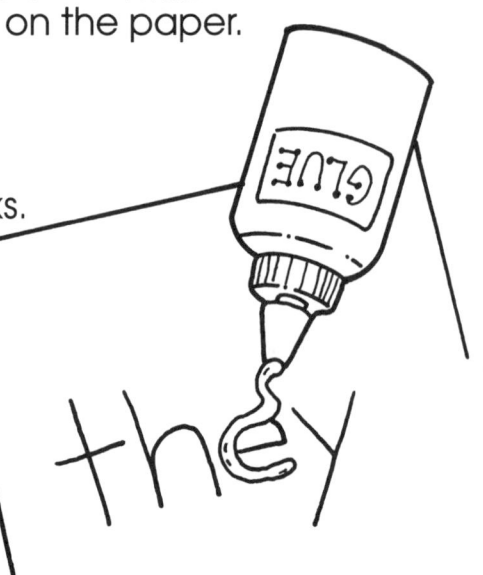

© Instructional Fair • TS Denison   IF5091 *Individualized Spelling–Primary*

teacher notes p. 7

Colored Vowels

Materials: a pencil, paper, and crayons, colored pencils, or markers

Directions:

1. Choose a spelling word. Say the word and write it in pencil on your paper.
2. Look at the word and decide which letters are vowels.
3. Using one crayon, trace each vowel in the word.
4. Repeat for each spelling word.

teacher notes p. 7

Cookie Cutters

Materials: play dough, a pencil, a rolling pin, a spatula, and alphabet cookie cutters

Directions:

1. Roll out the play dough.
2. Choose a spelling word. Say it.
3. Use the cookie cutters to cut out the letters of your chosen word.
4. Use the spatula to place the letters in the proper order.
5. Say the word and spell it to a friend.
6. Repeat for each spelling word.

teacher notes p. 7

Decorate It

Materials: 12" x 18" piece of drawing paper, pencil, and crayons, colored pencils, or markers

Directions:

1. Fold the paper in half three times.
2. Open your paper. You should have 8 boxes.
3. Choose a spelling word. Write it neatly at the top and bottom of the first box.
4. In the center of the box, write your word in large letters. You may write it fancy, doodle it, decorate it, or use the letters to make a picture.
5. Repeat for each word.

Dice-Roll Rainbow

teacher notes p. 7

Materials: a die, a pencil, paper, and crayons, markers, or colored pencils

Directions:

1. Choose a spelling word. Say it. Write the word in large letters on your paper.
2. Roll the die to determine how many crayons to use to decorate that word.
3. If you roll . . .

   1, choose 1 color.   4, choose 4 colors.
   2, choose 2 colors.   5, choose 5 colors.
   3, choose 3 colors.   6, choose 6 colors.

4. Trace the word with each color. For example, if you rolled 2, trace it with 2 colors. Complete the whole word with one color before using the next color.
5. Choose another spelling word and roll again!

teacher notes p. 7

Fabric Scraps

Materials: a marker, fabric scraps, and a piece of cardboard

Directions:

1. Place a fabric scrap over the cardboard.
2. Choose a spelling word. Say it.
3. Using the marker, write the spelling word neatly on the fabric.
4. Read the word. Trace the word three times with your pointer finger, saying each letter as you trace it. Repeat.

"*top, t-o-p, t-o-p, t-o-p; top, t-o-p, t-o-p, t-o-p*"

teacher notes p. 7

Fingerpaint Words

Materials: a large sheet of drawing paper, watercolor paints, a small container of water, and a pencil

Directions:

1. With a pencil, copy your spelling words onto the drawing paper in large letters. Make the letters large enough so you can trace over each letter using fingertips.
2. Choose a word. Say it.
3. Using the hand you write with, dip your fingertip in water. Then dip it into one color of paint.
4. Using your fingertip, trace over each letter in the word.
5. Wash the paint off your finger before changing to a different color.
6. Repeat for each of your spelling words.

teacher notes p. 7

Floor to Ceiling

Materials: index cards

Directions:

1. Write each of your spelling words on a card.
2. Choose a spelling card, lay it on the floor, and stand in front of it.
3. While still standing, close one eye and point to the spelling word on the floor. Say each letter as you "trace" it with your pointer finger.
4. Looking straight ahead, use your finger to write the spelling word in the air in front of you. You may glance back at the spelling card if necessary.
5. Pretend to change your finger into a pen with special ink that only you can see. "Write" the same word on the ceiling, saying each letter to yourself. Now your work is on the ceiling and you can look at it any time!
6. Now choose one more place in the room to "write" the word with your special ink.
7. Repeat for each of your spelling words.

teacher notes p. 7

Four-Column Spelling

Materials: lined writing paper and a pencil

Directions:

1. Fold the paper in half twice to make four columns.
2. Choose a spelling word. Say the word. Copy it on the first line in column one.
3. Copy the same word on the first line in column two.
4. Look at the word you wrote. Say it. Fold column one over column two.
5. With the first two columns hidden, write the same word on the first line in column three.
6. Open the folded paper and check your spelling in column three.
   a. If you spelled the word correctly, draw a star on the first line in column four.
   b. If you spelled the word incorrectly, draw a line under each correct letter in column three and write the word correctly in column four.
7. Repeat steps 2–6 with the rest of your spelling words, writing below the first word in each column.

© Instructional Fair • TS Denison IF5091 Individualized Spelling–Primary

teacher notes pp. 7–8

Four-Minute Spelling

Materials: a pencil, writing paper, and a timer

Directions:

1. Work with a partner. Set the timer for four minutes. Begin.
2. Say the first spelling word aloud. Then your partner writes it on a piece of paper.
3. If your partner spells it correctly, say the next word.
4. If the word is misspelled, show the word and have your partner write it three times correctly.
5. Repeat with all the words. When you complete the list, start over at the top of the list until four minutes are up.
6. Trade jobs and repeat steps 1–5.
7. Both partners count the number of words they spelled correctly in four minutes.
8. Add the totals together and try to top that number the next time.

teacher notes p. 8

Hands On!

Materials: a pencil and a pan full of something provided by your teacher

Directions:

1. Choose a word. Say it.
2. Use the index finger of your writing hand to write the word in your pan of stuff.
3. Find a partner and read and spell the word to him/her.
4. Repeat for each word.

© Instructional Fair • TS Denison   19   IF5091 *Individualized Spelling–Primary*

teacher notes p. 8

Jump Rope

Materials: a jump rope

Directions:

1. Choose a spelling word. Say the word.
2. Look at the word and decide which letters are consonants. You will jump on two feet for all consonants.
3. Decide which letters are vowels. You will jump on one foot for all vowels.
4. Say each letter of the word while jumping rope. Jump on two feet on consonants and on one foot for vowels.
5. Say the word again.
6. Repeat three times for each word.
7. Choose another spelling word and begin again.

"jump   j   –   u   –   m   –   p   jump"
         two feet one foot two feet two feet

teacher notes p. 8

Junk Mail Letters

Materials: junk mail, scissors, a pencil, envelope, and glue

Directions:

1. Write your name on the front of an empty junk mail envelope.
2. Write a spelling word on the back of the envelope.
3. Look through the junk mail for each letter in the spelling word. Cut out the letters and store in the envelope until you have found them all.
4. Put a thin line of glue on the back of the envelope under your spelling word.
5. Lay each letter on the glue in the correct order.
6. Repeat steps 2–5 for the rest of your spelling words.
7. When you are finished, show your work to a partner.

© Instructional Fair • TS Denison   20   IF5091 *Individualized Spelling–Primary*

teacher notes p. 8

Listening Center I

Making the tape

Materials: a blank cassette tape and a tape recorder

Directions:

1. Put the tape into the tape recorder.
2. Choose a word. Say it.
3. Practice spelling it out loud, touching each letter as you say it.
4. When you are ready, press the *record* button on the tape recorder.
5. Say the word clearly into the microphone. Silently count to ten. Say the word again and spell it out loud as you touch each letter.
6. Press the *stop* button on the tape recorder.
7. Choose another word and repeat steps 2–6.
8. Repeat for all of your spelling words, then rewind the tape.

Test yourself

Materials: a cassette tape of your spelling words (see above), lined paper, and a pencil

Directions:

1. Sit near the tape recorder with your paper and pencil. Put the cassette in the tape recorder and press the *play* button.
2. Listen to the first word. Write it quickly. Then touch each letter as the tape spells the word.
3. If you spelled the word correctly, star it. If incorrect, circle the word.
4. Continue with the rest of the recorded spelling words. When you are finished, rewind the tape.
5. Now look at the circled words. Find the correct spelling on your spelling list.
6. Write each circled word correctly three times.

© Instructional Fair • TS Denison — IF5091 *Individualized Spelling–Primary*

Listening Center II

teacher notes p. 8

Taping

Materials: a blank cassette tape and a tape recorder

Directions:

1. Put the tape into the tape recorder.
2. Choose a word. Say it.
3. Practice spelling it out loud, touching each letter as you say it.
4. When you are ready, press the *record* button on the tape recorder.
5. Say the word clearly into the microphone. Spell it slowly out loud as you touch each letter. Repeat the spelling three times. Say the word again.
6. Press the *stop* button on the tape recorder.
7. Choose another word and repeat steps 2–6.
8. Repeat for all of your spelling words, then rewind the tape.

Play It and Practice

Materials: a cassette tape of your spelling words (see above), lined paper, and a pencil

Directions:

1. Sit near the tape recorder with your paper and pencil. Put the cassette in the tape recorder and press the *play* button.
2. Write each spelling word as it is spelled on the tape recorder. Check your work as you listen.
3. When you are finished, rewind the tape.

© Instructional Fair • TS Denison   22   IF5091 *Individualized Spelling–Primary*

Magnetic Letters

teacher notes p. 8

Materials: a pencil and a set of magnetic letters

Directions:

1. Choose a spelling word. Say it.
2. Use the magnetic letters to spell the word on a metal surface.
3. Spell the word out loud three times, touching each letter as you say it.
4. Find a friend to listen and check your spelling.
5. Repeat for the rest of your spelling words.

Musical Spelling

teacher notes p. 8

Materials: a music maker, a pencil, and a crayon

Directions:

1. Write your spelling words with a pencil.
2. Trace all vowels with the crayon.
3. Choose two notes on the music maker: one for vowels and one for consonants.
4. Choose a spelling word. Say it.
5. Spell the word out loud. As you say a consonant, play the consonant note, and as you say a vowel, play the vowel note.
6. Repeat step 5 three times.
7. Repeat for each spelling word.

© Instructional Fair • TS Denison   23   IF5091 Individualized Spelling–Primary

teacher notes p. 8

Paint with Water

Materials: a paintbrush, a small container of water, and a chalkboard

Directions:

1. Choose a spelling word. Say it.
2. Dip your paintbrush in water. Paint each letter of the word on the chalkboard.
3. Check the spelling.
4. Read it to a partner.
5. Repeat for each word.

teacher notes p. 8

Paper Punch

Materials: 2" x 4" pieces of colored paper, a pencil, and a paper punch

Directions:

1. Choose a spelling word. Say it.
2. Copy the word on the colored paper in large letters. Check the spelling.
3. Use the paper punch to punch holes along the lines of the letters. Be sure to leave paper between each punch.
4. Spell the word three times, tracing each letter with your finger as you say it.
5. Repeat steps 1–4 for each spelling word.
6. Clean up the punched-out circles when you are done.

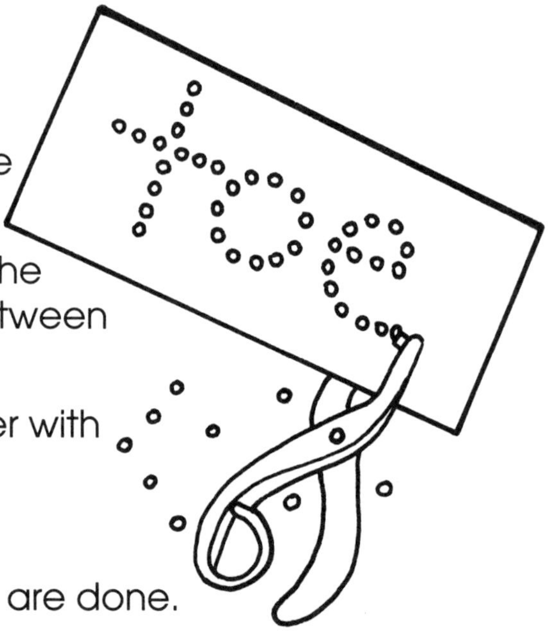

© Instructional Fair • TS Denison — IF5091 *Individualized Spelling–Primary*

teacher notes p. 9

Race to Draw

Materials: a pencil and paper

Directions: Before playing the game, decide on a simple character or picture you will draw. Be sure that partners agree on how many steps are required to draw the picture.

1. Partner A chooses a word from the list.
2. Partner A reads the word to partner B, uses it in a sentence, and then repeats the word.
3. Partner B writes the word on the paper.
4. Partner A checks the spelling.
5. If the word is spelled correctly, partner B may draw one part on his/her drawing.
6. If the spelling is incorrect, partner B must write the word two times correctly. Nothing is added to the drawing.
7. Partners switch jobs and repeat steps 1–6.
8. The game ends when one partner completes his/her picture.

teacher notes p. 9

Read, Write, and Spell

Materials: individual chalkboards, chalk, and erasers

Directions:

1. The leader says the word and writes it on a chalkboard.
2. The students say the word, write it on their chalkboards while they say each letter out loud, and then say the word again, "can, c - a - n, can."
3. The students say the word, spell it, and say it two more times.
4. The leader directs the students to lay down their chalk and hold up a pointer finger.
5. Students spell and say each word three times as they trace the letters with a finger.
6. The leader directs the students to erase their boards and write the spelling word at the top.
7. The leader checks each board for correct spelling.
8. Repeat steps 1–7 for each word.

© Instructional Fair • TS Denison — IF5091 *Individualized Spelling–Primary*

teacher notes p. 9

Sandpaper Spelling

Materials: sandpaper with the spelling words written on it

Directions:

1. Choose one sandpaper word. Say it.
2. Trace the word with your pointer finger.
3. Say each letter as you trace it.
4. Use the word you just traced in a sentence.
5. Share your sentence with someone.
6. Repeat for each spelling word.

teacher notes p. 9

Scrambled Words

Materials: blank cards, a pencil, and writing paper

Directions:

1. Choose a spelling word. Say it.
2. Write it on a card and underline it.
3. On a separate piece of paper, scramble the letters of the spelling word. Be sure to include all of the letters.
4. Write the scrambled word neatly on the back of the card.
5. On each new card, repeat steps 1–4 until you have used all of your spelling words.
6. Share your cards with a partner.
7. Your partner should look at the scrambled side, unscramble the word, and write it on a separate paper.
8. He/she can check for the correct spelling on the back of the card.

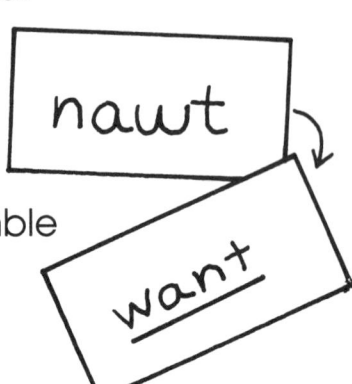

teacher notes p. 9

Scramble, Unscramble I

Materials: grid paper (p. 48), a pencil, a dark crayon, scissors, and an envelope

Directions:

1. Choose a spelling word. Say it.
2. Write it on grid paper—one letter per box.
3. Check your spelling. If it is correct, trace each letter with a dark crayon.
4. Repeat for each spelling word.
5. Cut out each box with a letter in it.
6. Place the letters inside the envelope.

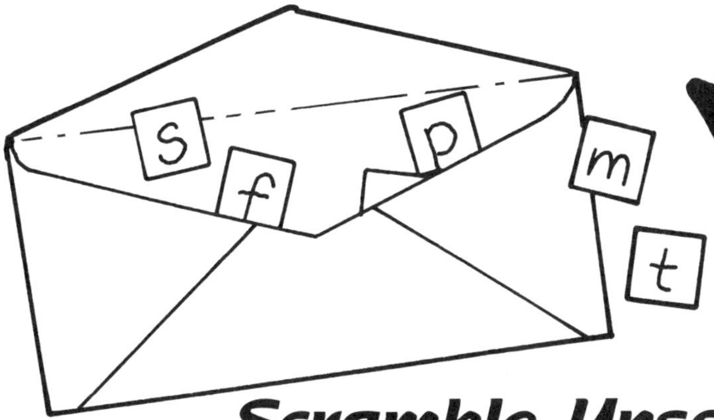

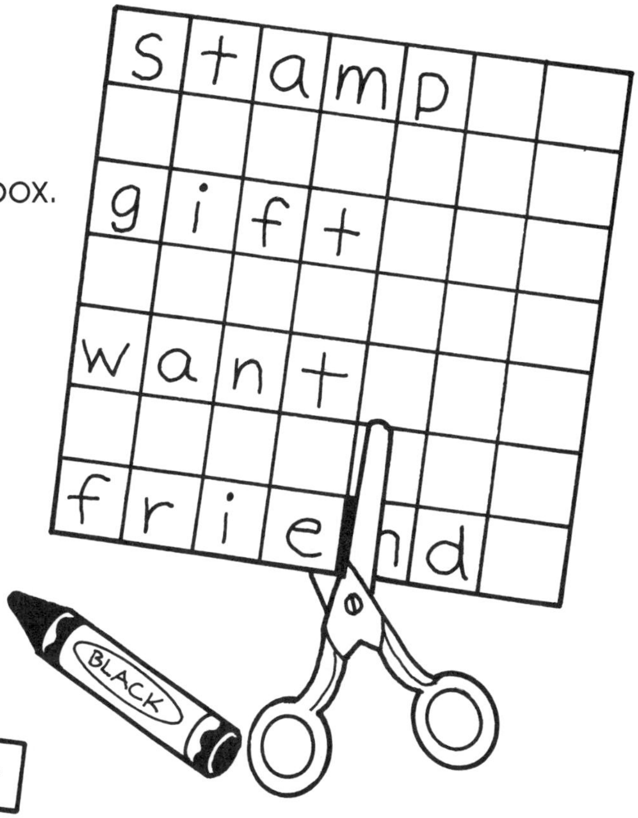

teacher notes p. 9

Scramble, Unscramble II

Materials: an envelope of scrambled letters and a pencil

Directions:

1. Dump out the letters from the envelope.
2. Use these letters to spell each of your words.
3. When you are finished, share your work with a partner.
4. Say each word. Point to each letter as you spell the word. Say each word again.

© Instructional Fair • TS Denison   27   IF5091 *Individualized Spelling–Primary*

teacher notes p. 9

Sidewalk Chalk

Materials: chalk and a section of sidewalk

Directions:

1. Choose a spelling word. Say it.
2. Copy the word onto the sidewalk with your chalk. Say the word.
3. Write the word three times. Say and spell the word each time you write it.
4. Choose another word and repeat the directions.

teacher notes p. 9

Silly Voices

Materials: your voice

Directions:

1. Choose a spelling word.
2. Use your happy voice to say the word, spell it, and say it again.
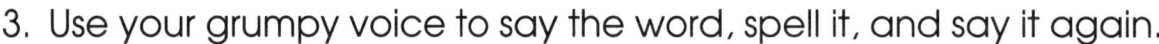
   "and   a-n-d   and"
3. Use your grumpy voice to say the word, spell it, and say it again.
4. Use your surprised voice to say the word, spell it, and say it again.
5. Choose two more voices and say the word, spell it, and say it again. Some voice suggestions include cackly, angry, sad, whiny, soothing, whispery, and disgusted.
6. Say and spell the rest of your spelling words in a variety of voices.

© Instructional Fair • TS Denison   28   IF5091 *Individualized Spelling–Primary*

teacher notes p. 9

Snakes and Worms

Materials: play dough

Directions:

1. Make long snakes and skinny worms out of the dough.
2. Choose a spelling word. Say it.
3. Use your snakes and worms to form each of the letters in this word.
4. Read the word. Say each letter as you touch it.
5. Read and spell your word to someone.
6. Repeat steps 2–5 to practice the rest of your spelling words.

teacher notes p. 9

Spelling Cards

Materials: a pencil, dark crayon, and one card for each spelling word

Directions:

1. Choose a spelling word. With a pencil, copy the word in large letters on the card.
2. Check the spelling of your word.
3. Trace the word with the dark crayon several times.
4. Rub your pointer finger over the letters as you spell the word out loud three times.
5. Repeat for each spelling word.

teacher notes p. 9

Spelling Stairs

Materials: grid paper (p. 48) and a pencil

Directions:

1. Choose a spelling word. Say the word.
2. Write the first letter of the spelling word in a box on the first line.
3. Directly below the first letter, write the first and second letters of the word in two boxes.
4. Write the first, second, and third letters of the word in three boxes on the third line.
5. Write the first, second, third, and fourth letters of the word in four boxes on the fourth line.
6. Continue until the full word is written. You have made a staircase out of this word. Count how many steps this word has and write the number at the top of the steps.
7. Repeat to make steps out of the rest of your spelling words.

teacher notes p. 10

Spiral It

Materials: drawing paper, pencil, and crayons

Directions:

1. Choose a spelling word. Say it.
2. Use your pencil to write the word in large letters.
3. Check the spelling.
4. Use a crayon to draw spirals on each letter.
5. Say and spell the word three times.
6. Repeat for each word.

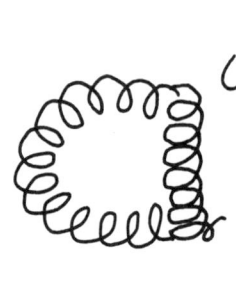

© Instructional Fair • TS Denison   IF5091 *Individualized Spelling–Primary*

teacher notes p. 10

Squirt Bottle

Materials: your spelling list, a squirt bottle filled with water, and a large section of sidewalk

Directions:

1. Choose a spelling word. Say it out loud.
2. Spell it out loud while looking at your list and then say the word again.
3. Use your squirt bottle to write your spelling word in water on the sidewalk.
4. Before the word dries, check the spelling of the word.
5. Repeat for each word.

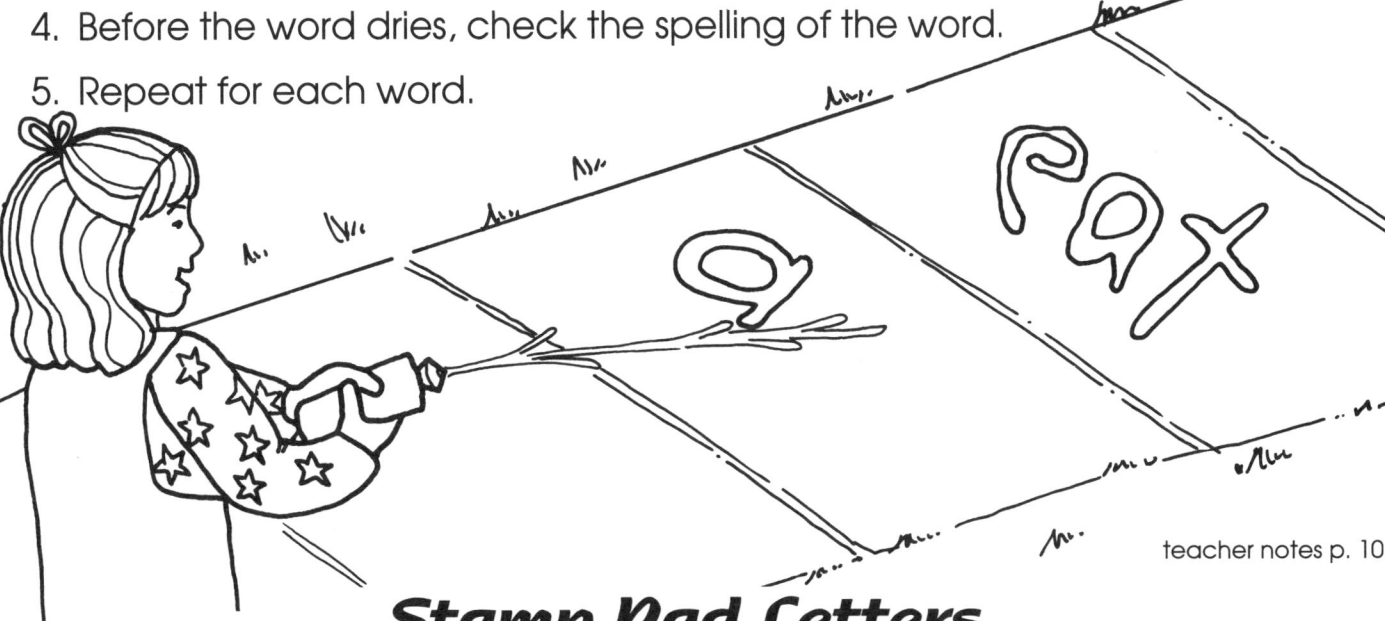

teacher notes p. 10

Stamp Pad Letters

Materials: paper, a pencil, a stamp pad, your spelling list, and alphabet stamps

Directions:

1. Choose a spelling word. Say it.
2. Write it on your paper with a pencil. Each letter should be about the same size as the stamp letters. Check your spelling.
3. Using the alphabet stamps, stamp each letter of the word under the spelling word you wrote.
4. Check the spelling of the word.
5. Repeat for each spelling word.

© Instructional Fair • TS Denison   31   IF5091 *Individualized Spelling–Primary*

teacher notes p. 10

String It Along

Materials: several pieces of string

Directions:

1. Choose a spelling word. Say it.
2. Form each letter of the word with a piece of string.
3. After you have spelled the word with string, read it to a partner.
4. Say the word. Point to each letter as you say it. Say the word again.
5. Read and spell the word to someone.
6. Repeat for each of your spelling words.

teacher notes p. 10

Texture Writing

Materials: a crayon, drawing paper, and a textured surface

Directions:

1. Place your paper over the textured surface.
2. Choose one of your words. Say it.
3. Using a crayon, write the word on the paper in large letters. Say each letter as you write it.
4. Put your crayon down. Trace the letters on your paper with your finger.
5. Remove your paper from the textured surface.
6. Now use your finger to "write" the word on the textured surface. It is invisible!
7. Say each letter as you write it.
8. Choose another word and repeat steps 1–7.

Typewriter

teacher notes p. 10

Materials: paper and a typewriter

Directions:

1. Feed the paper into the typewriter.
2. Choose a word. Say it.
3. Type the word and check your spelling.
4. Type the word correctly three times. If you make a mistake, type the word again.
5. Type each of your spelling words in the same manner.

teacher notes p. 10

Word Shapes

Materials: grid paper (p. 48) and a pencil

There are three different grid-paper shapes for lowercase letters.

One box letters: **a, c, e, i, m, n, o, r, s, u, v, w, x, z**

One box and the box above letters: **b, d, f, h, k, l, t**

One box and the box below letters: **g, j, p, q, y**

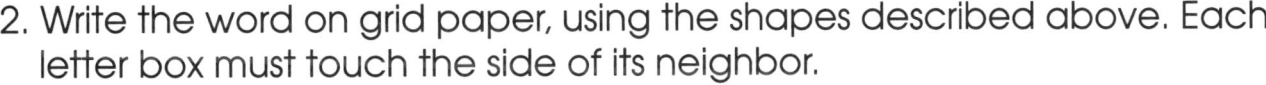

Directions:

1. Choose a spelling word. Say it.
2. Write the word on grid paper, using the shapes described above. Each letter box must touch the side of its neighbor.
3. Trace around the outside edge of the boxes that contain the word.
4. On another sheet of grid paper, copy the shape of the word without the letters written inside.
5. Repeat for each word.
6. Save the sheet that has empty shapes to use on another day or trade with a friend. Then fill in the empty boxes with the spelling word that has that shape.

teacher notes p. 10

Write It on . . .

Materials: a pencil and your choice of paper

Directions:

1. Choose a word. Say it.
2. Write the word on your paper. Say the word.
3. Write the word four times, saying each letter as you spell it.
4. Repeat for each word.

teacher notes p. 10

Write It with . . .

Materials: lined paper, a pencil, and three other writing tools

Directions:

1. Fold your paper in half lengthwise twice to form 4 columns.
2. Choose a word. Say it.
3. Write the word with your pencil in the first column. Check the spelling.
4. Choose a different writing tool to write the same word in column two.
5. Choose a third writing tool to write the same word in column three.
6. Choose a final writing tool to write the word in column four.
7. Repeat steps 2–6 for each word.

© Instructional Fair • TS Denison   34   IF5091 *Individualized Spelling–Primary*

Writing on the Wall

teacher notes p. 10

Materials: an overhead projector, a transparency, and an overhead pen

Directions:

1. Choose a spelling word. Say it.
2. Write it neatly on the overhead transparency. Check your spelling.
3. Write the word three times.
4. Repeat for each of your spelling words.

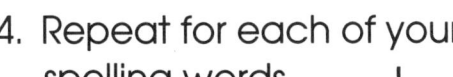

Notes to the teacher
Context-Based Activities

The following activities provide opportunities for the students to go beyond repetition and use the spelling words in meaningful contexts. Use at least one of these activities with each word every week. The information below will help you choose and prepare the best activities for your students and refer you to the corresponding sheet of student directions. For each activity, every student will need a copy of his/her spelling list or the Weekly Recording Chart (p. 42).

- **ABC** (p. 37) uses spelling words to practice alphabetical order. Discuss what to do with words that have the same first letter or first group of letters before students work independently. Having the words on cards allows students to easily move the words around before committing the word order to paper.

- **Dictionary Cards and Sentences** (p. 37) provides students with the correct spellings of their words along with a sentence with which to associate each word. You may wish to have beginning spellers dictate their sentence to you or a volunteer. This activity links spelling with reading since it provides a context and a relevant piece of reading. Teach the students how to file the cards in alphabetical order in their storage boxes. Store dictionary cards in purchased file boxes or boxes made from tagboard or the bottom of cereal or cake mix boxes, or simply wrap with a rubber band. Cut or purchase cards to fit the container. Some printing companies are willing to give schools scraps of paper that work well for this purpose.

If your students need to dictate their sentences, use parent or other volunteers, older student helpers, or more capable students within the classroom. Or, if a small group of students agrees upon a sentence, you can write it on the board for the group to copy.

- **Flip-Check** (p. 38) places the spelling words in the context of a student-written sentence. Students first create the flip-check flashcards; then they use them for a quick, self-check of their spelling. Make a sample prior to assigning this activity to show students how to cover the spelling word and cut the flip-checks. For younger learners, the teacher or volunteer should make the cards. Then let the students draw a picture of the word or dictate the sentence.

- **Flip Up, Fill in the Blank** (p. 38) provides students with the opportunity to write and edit complete sentences and then see each spelling word in a meaningful context for practice. If you don't have sentence-strip paper, cut 12" x 18" paper into 2" x 18" strips. Also provide paper (approx. 2" x 4") to cover the spelling word. Demonstrate how to cut and glue a flip tab over a word prior to assigning this as an independent activity.

After creating the sentences with the hidden spelling words, students can share them or practice on their own sentence strips.

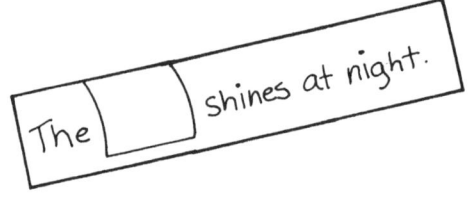

- **Photo Captions** (p. 39) requires high-level thinking. Students must find appropriate pictures and then write a related sentence. This gives students experience in writing descriptively and paying attention to details. Sources for photos include old magazines, advertising inserts, newspapers, and old books. Students could draw their own pictures as well.

Extension: Locate a photo and write about it using all of the spelling words.

- **Relationships** (p. 39) requires students to study the letters of each spelling word and relate them to words they already know how to read or spell. If the student identifies the double *t* in *better* or the *co* in *come*, they are more likely to remember these letters when it is time to take the test. Seeing the *co* in *come* and identifying it with the *co* in *cold* helps the child spell the word even if the letters are pronounced differently.

- **Teach a Word** (p. 40) is an activity of higher-level thinking that requires students to analyze each word and decide how to teach it to a group of students. Teaching others is one of the best ways to retain information. Divide the spelling words between the members of each participating group. Each student is responsible for teaching their portion of the list to the group. To learn the complete list, they must work together. This may be an appropriate activity before the pretest.

teacher notes p. 36

ABC

Materials: blank index cards (or the cards from **Dictionary Cards and Sentences**—below), lined paper, and a pencil

Directions:

1. Write one spelling word on each card. Or use your cards from **Dictionary Cards and Sentences.**

2. Choose two cards and look at the first letter of each word. Decide which letter is closer to the beginning of the alphabet. Place the cards in order on the table.

3. Choose a third card. Compare the first letter to the first letters on the other two cards. Lay the card down in alphabetical order.

4. Repeat for each spelling word.

5. When all of the words are in alphabetical order, write them in order on the paper.

teacher notes p. 36

Dictionary Cards and Sentences

Materials: precut cards, a pencil, and a storage box

Directions:

1. Choose a spelling word. Say it.

2. Write the spelling word neatly on one side of the card.

3. On the back of the card, write a sentence using this spelling word.

4. Underline the spelling word in the sentence.

5. Read the sentence to a partner.

6. Repeat for each word.

7. Put your spelling words in your storage box in alphabetical order.

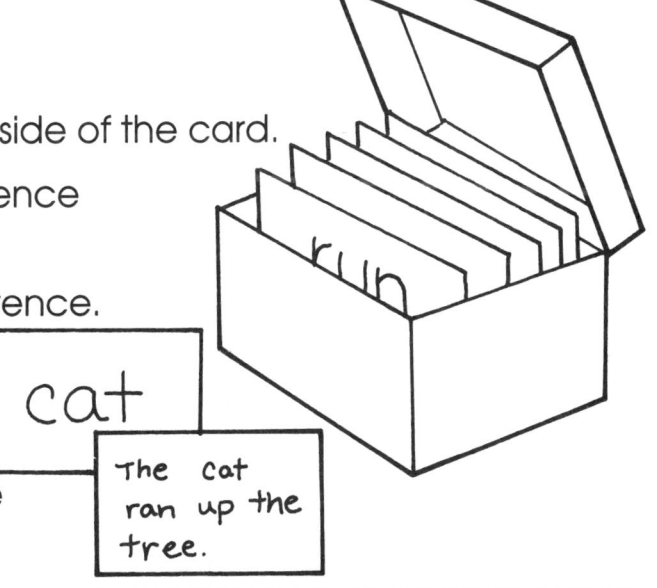

© Instructional Fair • TS Denison 37 IF5091 *Individualized Spelling–Primary*

Flip-Check

teacher notes p. 36

Materials: grid paper (p. 48), a pencil, 3" x 5" index cards, a dark crayon, scissors, glue

Directions:

1. Choose a spelling word. Write it neatly on the grid paper, one letter per box.
2. Check your spelling. Then, trace each letter with the dark crayon.
3. Cut out the word and the squares above each letter. Fold the top boxes down over the word. Glue the word to the bottom of the index card.
4. Now cut along the vertical lines of the top boxes so that each letter has its own flip-tab.
5. In the space above the word, either draw a picture that shows the meaning of the word or write a sentence using the word.
6. Repeat for each spelling word.
7. Use the flashcards to practice spelling words. Look at the picture or read the sentence and write the spelling word on a separate sheet of paper. Lift a tab if you need help. Check your spelling when you have finished the word.

Flip Up, Fill in the Blank

teacher notes p. 36

Materials: practice paper, sentence-strip paper, scrap paper, and glue

Directions:

1. Choose a spelling word. Write a sentence using the spelling word. Underline the spelling word.
2. Have someone edit your sentence.
3. Repeat for each spelling word.
4. Write one edited sentence on a sentence strip.
5. Cut a rectangle of scrap paper to cover the spelling word. Glue the paper over the spelling word along the top edge so it can be flipped up to show the word beneath.
6. Repeat for each edited sentence.
7. To practice spelling, read a sentence and write the hidden word on a separate paper. Lift the flap to check your spelling.

© Instructional Fair • TS Denison   IF5091 *Individualized Spelling–Primary*

Photo Captions

teacher notes p. 36

Materials: drawing paper, lined paper, a pencil, scissors, glue, and old magazines for cutting

Directions:

1. Read your spelling list. Think of ways to use these words in sentences.
2. Cut out or draw a picture which is connected in some way to one of your spelling words.
3. Glue the picture on the drawing paper, leaving space for a sentence.
4. On a piece of lined paper, write a sentence about the photo including one or more of your spelling words. Have someone help you edit the sentence.
5. Neatly rewrite the sentence on the drawing paper.
6. Underline any spelling words used in your sentence.
7. Repeat steps 2–6 until you have used each of your spelling words.

Relationships

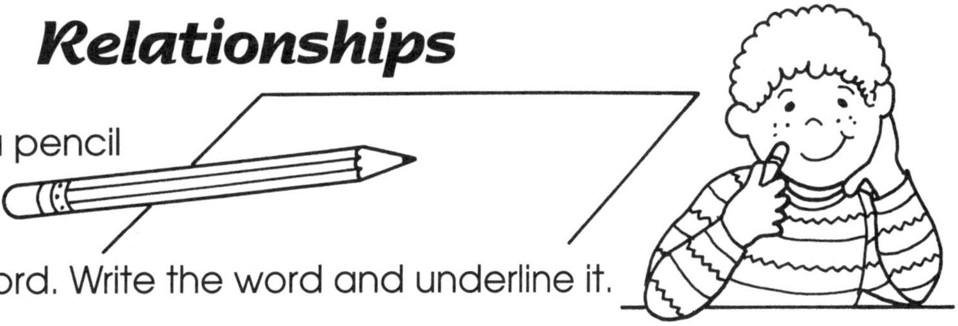

Materials: paper and a pencil

Directions:

1. Choose a spelling word. Write the word and underline it.
2. Study the word and decide if there is any part of the word that is the same in another word you know.
3. Write the related word and underline the part that is the same.
4. Write at least one more word that is related to your spelling word.

    Examples: <u>better</u>: <u>bet</u>, <u>butter</u>, and <u>flutter</u>

    <u>come</u>: <u>com</u>b, <u>came</u>, <u>co</u>at, <u>cor</u>n, and <u>co</u>ld

5. Repeat for each spelling word.

teacher notes p. 36

Teach a Word

Materials: a spelling list shared between group members, a recording chart, and a pencil

Directions:

1. This is a group activity. Choose a leader.
2. The leader chooses a word and decides how best to teach it to the others in the group.
3. The leader teaches the word to the group. The leader says the word, gives spelling tips, and says the word again.

    Example: peninsula, p-e-n as in <u>pen</u>, i-n as in <u>in</u>, just remember s-u-l-a, peninsula

4. Each group member repeats the spelling three times, then writes the word on their recording chart.
5. The leader checks each group member's spelling of the word on his/her chart.
6. The leader chooses a different person to teach another word.
7. Repeat steps 1–4 until all words have been taught.

© Instructional Fair • TS Denison   40   IF5091 *Individualized Spelling–Primary*

Management

Use the following activities and charts to manage the daily work of your individualized spelling program.

Pretesting allows students to feel satisfaction for words already mastered and to be aware of which words they need to practice. The pretest is the initial activity of the week. A pretest can be given by the teacher to the whole group, by a volunteer to a small group or an individual student, or by one student to another student. Give students full credit for any words spelled correctly on the pretest, and then allow them to develop their own list of words. You may wish to use copies of **Spelling Test** (p.45) instead of regular lined paper.

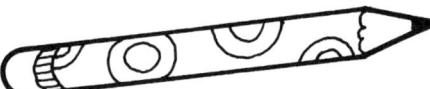

Pretest

Materials: a pencil and lined paper

Directions:

1. Work with a partner. The person being tested should fold a paper in half lengthwise to make two columns.

2. The test giver chooses one word from his/her partner's list.

3. The test giver says the word clearly and uses it in a sentence.

4. The person being tested writes tthe word in the first column of his/her paper.

5. Repeat for each spelling word.

6. When the pretest is finished, switch roles and follow the same procedure.

To correct the pretest:

1. Each partner copies his/her spelling words in the right column next to his/her pretest words.

2. He/she compares the pretest words to the copied words.

   a) If the word is correct, he/she underlines it and draws a star next to it.

   b) If the word is not correct, he/she underlines each correct letter. Then he/she circles the word.

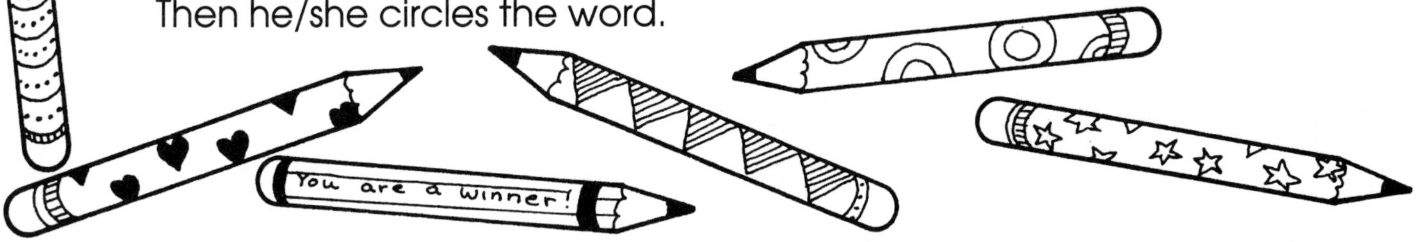

I Know These Words provides a location for students to list spelling words successfully learned. Use a spiral notebook, stapled or bound writing paper, 5" x 7" cards bound with a ring, or paper in a folder. On each page, write a letter of the alphabet, in order. On the cover, write **I Know These Words**. As words qualify for entry into the **I Know These Words** booklet or cards, write the word on the corresponding page.

I Know These Words

Materials: a pencil and your "I Know These Words" booklet

Directions:

1. Look at the first letter of the word you are going to enter in your word booklet.
2. Find the page that has the same letter on it.
3. Write the new word neatly on the page. Say it.
4. Read the other words on the page.
5. Notice how your word booklet is filling up!
6. Repeat for each word you enter.

Management

Name _____ Date _____

Daily Recording Chart

Write your spelling words on the lines. When you complete an activity, check the space in front of the word.

Activity _____

My list of words:

___ 1. _____   ___ 7. _____

___ 2. _____   ___ 8. _____

___ 3. _____   ___ 9. _____

___ 4. _____   ___ 10. _____

___ 5. _____   ___ 11. _____

___ 6. _____   ___ 12. _____

Spelling Words to Practice

Write the words on this list that need extra practice for the spelling test.

Activity _____

___ 1. _____   ___ 7. _____

___ 2. _____   ___ 8. _____

___ 3. _____   ___ 9. _____

___ 4. _____   ___ 10. _____

___ 5. _____   ___ 11. _____

___ 6. _____   ___ 12. _____

© Instructional Fair • TS Denison   IF5091 *Individualized Spelling–Primary*

Management

Name _____ Week of _____

Weekly Recording Chart

Write your spelling words on the numbered lines. Refer to the activity choices at the bottom of the page by letter. After using a spelling activity, write the letter of the activity on the first available small line after the spelling word.

1. _____ ___ ___ ___
2. _____ ___ ___ ___
3. _____ ___ ___ ___
4. _____ ___ ___ ___
5. _____ ___ ___ ___
6. _____ ___ ___ ___

7. _____ ___ ___ ___
8. _____ ___ ___ ___
9. _____ ___ ___ ___
10. _____ ___ ___ ___
11. _____ ___ ___ ___
12. _____ ___ ___ ___

Activity Choices

A. _____
B. _____
C. _____
D. _____
E. _____

F. _____
G. _____
H. _____
I. _____
J. _____

© Instructional Fair • TS Denison   IF5091 *Individualized Spelling–Primary*

Management

Name _____   **Week of** _____

Spelling Test

Management

Name _____   Test on _____

My Spelling List